Highlights

Hidden Pictures Dinosaur Puffy Sticker Playscenes

**Find 8 hidden objects in each scene.
Then use your stickers to decorate!**

Illustrated by Patrick Girouard, Kelly Kennedy, Dave Klug, and Neil Numberman

HIGHLIGHTS PRESS
Honesdale, Pennsylvania

Game On!

Zelda and Mario are racing each other in their new video game.

Objects to Find

 **Tennis Ball**

 Envelope

 Camera

 Muffin

 Comb

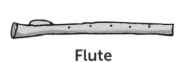 **Flute**

 **Artist's Brush**

 Mitten

Imagine and Draw

What game would you like to play with a dinosaur? Draw a picture of it here.

Say "Cheese"!

The Rex family is having a blast on their family vacation.

Objects to Find

Comb

Hammer

Mug

Hairbrush

Spoon

Feather

Tack

Feather
Duster

Make a Match
Find three pairs of matching postcards.

Dino Dance

Watch out for dipping dinosaurs!

Objects to Find

Lollipop

Slice of Watermelon

Envelope

Candy Corn

Saltshaker

Sock

Fried Egg

Oar

Find Your Way

Lead the conga line through the dance floor.

Construction Crew

These dinosaurs are hard at work building Paleontologist Plaza.

Objects to Find

Diamond

Plunger

Wedge of Orange

Spoon

Crown

Domino

Pencil

Hairbrush

Imagine and Draw

What's being built on this lot? Draw a picture of it here.

A Night at the Museum

Who is brave enough to put their sleeping bag next to *T. rex*?

Objects to Find

Spoon

Frying Pan

Snail

Sock

Adhesive Bandage

Paper Clip

Banana

Ruler

Make a Match

Find three pairs of matching fossils.

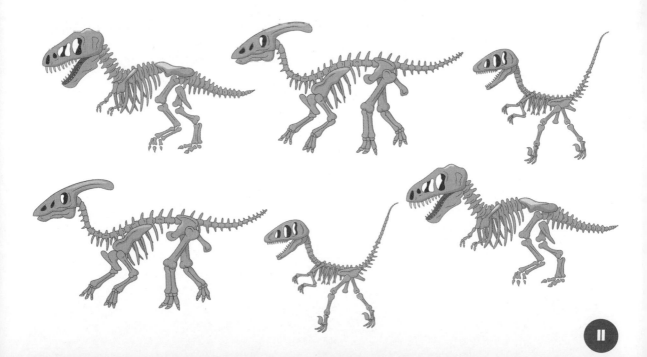

Hungry Hungry Herbivores

Good thing the salad bar is stocked!

Objects to Find

Slice of Pie

Sailboat

Envelope

Crescent Moon

Flashlight

Lollipop

Crown

Fish

Find Your Way

Follow each path to find out which dinosaur will sit at which table.

Objects to Find

Flashlight

Funnel

Dog Bone

Fried Egg

Pencil

Hat

Wishbone

Heart

Imagine and Draw
Who or what is swimming in this prehistoric pond?

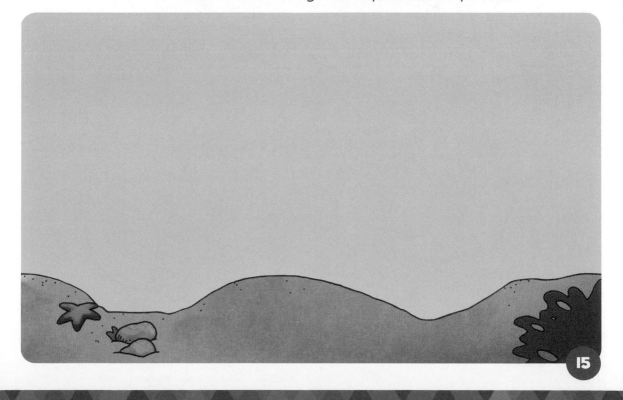

A Ton of Fun

What's your favorite classroom activity?

Objects to Find

Bell

Comb

Ring

Fan

Ruler

Gift

Fishhook

Wedge of Orange

Make a Match

Find three pairs of matching easels.

Dino Dinner

This *Stegosaurus*'s plates are full!

Objects to Find

House

Comb

Lollipop

Boomerang

Flute

Ring

Toothbrush

Fish

Find Your Way

Help Declan find the way to his friend's house.

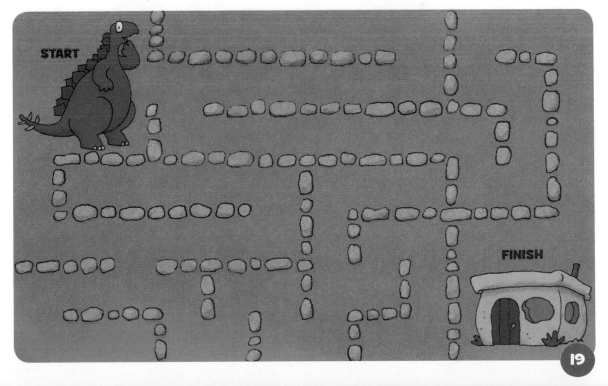

Open Wide!

Sue is getting all 60 of her teeth checked at this dentist appointment.

Objects to Find

Crescent Moon

Saucepan

Chili Pepper

Binoculars

Ruler

Comb

Shoe

Mug

Imagine and Draw

What did these parrot paleontologists dig up? Draw a picture of it here.

Tug of ROAR

It's field day at Stonyrock School.

Objects to Find

Tack

Scissors

Comb

Banana

Slice of
Pizza

Boomerang

Mitten

Drumstick

Make a Match

Find three pairs of matching dinosaurs.

Velociraptor Victory

Victor won the race!

Objects to Find

Vase

Van

Violin

Valentine

Volcano

Volleyball

Vial

Vest

Find Your Way

Help Vivien find her way to the finish line.

"Tag, You're It!"

Benjamin and his friends are playing the day away.

Objects to Find

Envelope

Baseball

Glove

Piece of Popcorn

Mitten

Toothbrush

Cinnamon Bun

Bell

Imagine and Draw
What stars do these dinos see?

That's Pre-hysterical!

Sara the *Parasaurolophus* has the entire audience laughing.

Objects to Find

Spoon

Canoe

Banana

Pencil

Hammer

Fish

Spatula

Tack

Make a Match

Find three pairs of matching dinosaurs.

Jurassic Parkas

Bailey needs a *looooooong* scarf to fit her neck.

Objects to Find

Comb

Pear

Envelope

Marshmallow

Slice of
Pizza

Mug

Caterpillar

Arrowhead

Find Your Way

Which hat belongs to which dinosaur?

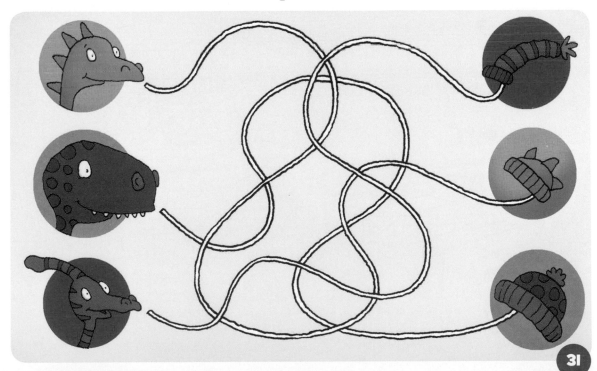

Happy Birthday, Spike!

A birthday party 100 million years in the making . . .

Objects to Find

Lollipop

Wedge of Lime

Envelope

Magnet

Artist's Brush

Adhesive Bandage

Doughnut

Mitten

Imagine and Draw

What birthday gift would you give to a dinosaur? Draw a picture of it here.

Museum of Natural History

What an awesome field trip!

Objects to Find

Slice of Bread

Bowling Pin

Paper Airplane

Horseshoe

Wristwatch

Light Bulb

Hanger

Vase

Make a Match

Find three pairs of matching fossils.

Touchdown!

The Terrific Triceratops are up by 7 points.

Objects to Find

Banana

Ice-Cream Bar

Canoe

Worm

Bowl

Ruler

Nail

Croissant

Find Your Way

Help Cameron find his way to the end zone.

START

FINISH

Scrub-a-Dub

Why do all the bubbles keep popping?

Objects to Find

Crescent Moon

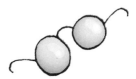

Eyeglasses

Hat

Slice of Pizza

Egg

Worm

Button

Snowman

Imagine and Draw

What's floating in this tub? Draw a picture of them here.

Tea, Rex?

Afternoon is the perfect time for a cuppa.

Objects to Find

Tent

Trowel

Tomato

Telescope

Tweezers

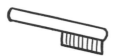
Toothbrush

Tennis Ball

Toy Top

Make a Match

Find three pairs of matching teacups.

Objects to Find

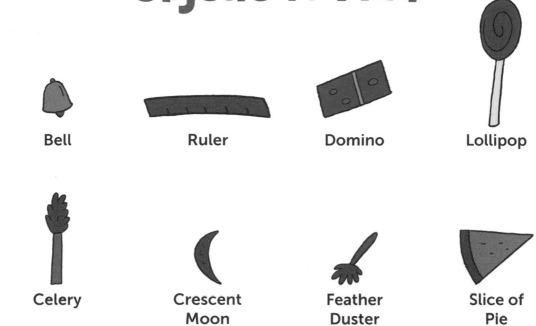

Bell

Ruler

Domino

Lollipop

Celery

Crescent Moon

Feather Duster

Slice of Pie

Find Your Way

Help Daisy meet up with her friends.

START

FINISH

Good Morning!

Dakota was up before sunrise this morning.

Objects to Find

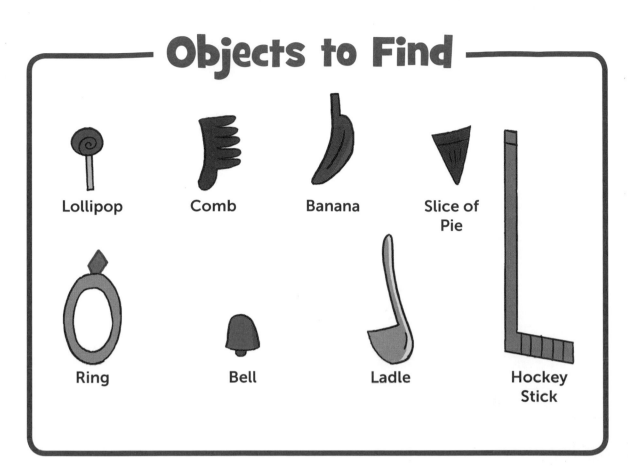

Lollipop

Comb

Banana

Slice of Pie

Ring

Bell

Ladle

Hockey Stick

Imagine and Draw

Draw a picture of what you see out your window in the morning.

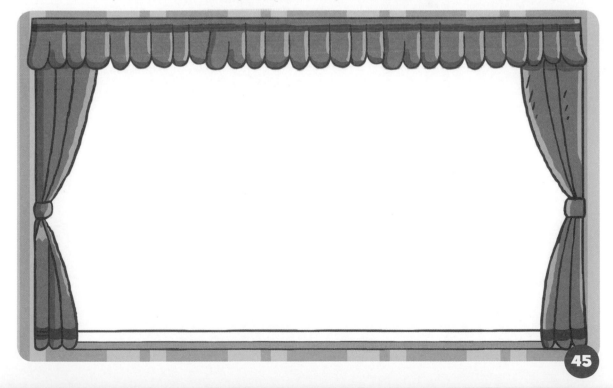

Answers

Page 2

Pages 4–5

Pages 6–7

Page 8

Pages 10–11

Pages 12–13

Page 14

Pages 16–17

Answers

Pages 18-19

Page 20

Pages 22-23

Pages 24-25

 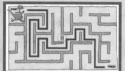

Page 26

Pages 28-29

Pages 30-31

Page 32

Answers

Pages 34–35

Pages 36–37

Page 38

Pages 40–41

Pages 42–43

Page 44

For information about permission to reprint selections
from this book, please contact permissions@highlights.com.

Published by Highlights Press
815 Church Street
Honesdale, Pennsylvania 18431
Printed in Humen Town, Dongguan City, China;
Stickers manufactured in Huizhou, Guangdong, China.
12/2020
ISBN: 978-1-64472-114-8

First edition
Visit our website at Highlights.com.
10 9 8 7 6 5 4

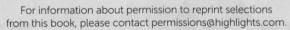